Beautiful Disorder

poetry

Wm. Anthony Connolly

BookLeaf
Publishing

India | USA | UK

Dedication

For Dyan

Preface

I write every day, something, anything, in a journal or a typed sheet of paper on a manual typewriter. Most items chronicled on paper never see the light of day; no one else reads them. But what they do see is me, if not daily, then occasionally, which is fine. They -- whoever they are -- see the public me and sometimes the private one. My daily page, which I call *The Daily Museum of Agitation Pages,* is a ledger of my weather, physically, yes, but mostly mentally. Getting it down makes me understand the world and my place in it. These poems are a snapshot (of the so-called agitation pages) into this daily struggle to find solace and maintain wonder in the belief that beauty will save the world (Dostoevsky might have said that). The poems are not formal, per se, although some are an attempted form, but rather lines of my sense of how it, the world and us in it, lies, and what is required to do next. I believe in the resiliency of words, the beautiful disorder of poetry (Theodore Roethke), and the power of faith.

All the best,
Anthony
Delaware 2025

Acknowledgements

None of the poems of *Beautiful Disorder* have been previously published, although some have been posted through social media, albeit in slightly different versions.

Pancake

This is the pancake
A first poem to take
You and hopefully digest well
Even though it's burnt to hell

It is to say, hey
I'm not perfect, okay
Some of these you will like
Others can just take a hike

But be kind if you can
This poet is merely a man
Who speaks to dogs and plants
Writes poems and rants

In a bathrobe with typewriter
Just to make life a little brighter
So, enjoy what you may
Surely it won't ruin your day

My dogs love these poems
Plants don't read they skim

Here we are – away we go
This is my book, my show!

Glimmer

Zigzag stirring amble of forgetful mind,
Fading echoes whisper secrets left behind.
Shadows strafe this sortie of time,
And soul's wisp once still, wanders, lost in wartime.
Through forests dark where love and hope did shine,
A faint fuse flickers, as if divine.
Yet still I fumble, though paths twist and decline,
For in the gone, a glimmer of once was mine.
Dream-like it disperses at a dutiful dawn,
Absent moments haunt and never are reborn.
Tears fall blurring my lonely gaze,
Longing to find what once called its dorm.
And still I roam, lost – forever to remain,
Lost – yet searching still, love's utter domain.

&

Socks
& the will to care about songbird migration
Keys
& the power to change the Web's view of me
Memories
& the smell of absinthe before I got sober
Magic
& a map with specific directions written in red
A pony
& a long story about a short incident
One right shoe
& the left, because hey why not
Queen of Cups
& the inability to calculate the number of burnt bridges
Cords
& how we once gathered round a blazing fire
Books
& the narrative of the Sun king before Gilgamesh
Hats
& some of my father's hair

Could and Oughts

While at the library
Amid spines of odyssey
Lost in so many thoughts
Wishes, coulds and oughts

Dewey decimal drudgery
Covers of blue imagery
I was to write books
Every author in their nooks

These days the aisles fill
Where old talks rattle still
Promises made aloud
The vouchsafe of the proud

My words only in mind
Mine and sometimes fine
The creative life remains
Green fuse through my veins

Not upon a shelf
Still alive with the self

Summer's End

Nu scilun herga hefenricaes uard

and the Pool-Cleaner skims dead leaves, bees
Beatles — *she loves you-ya, ya, ya...* — fading
Down the street a Marine, in full dress, home
Before he leaves, hoists a tan, blonde-hair sister.

Coolness has gilded the air
Sky one folding and unfolding flag of worn holey
Shimmer and surrender. Leaves and wind whispering
Summer doesn't know it's terminal.

No rituals now until the season of the dead
Return seeking last-minute departure gifts
Clothed in the patina of the fall, fire and ash
Green at being so cold, they chant, they moan

At my door disguised as sprogs, to ease their pain
And mine. Amid this exuent parade always one
Or two of the missing. Staying out of way, still
Lingering, a shiver down

Turning back — not all the way;

Soon enough with the coming
Of winter and endless Keeper hosannas, for being here
Through the season of dying, which seems so pure
Longing buds for burning halcyon days.

She loves you-ya, ya, ya...

Bees, leaves.

Status Updates

1.
Pruning roses
Easy poetry to weave
Through thorns dead
Branches once enjambed
With beauty beyond
Words
And the occasional
Prick scratch
To remind one of life's
Duality blood
And bloom

2.
The anniversary narrative
Thread reads strong through
Sickness and health
Poverty and wealth
Over the years of being
Together connected in loving
Each other as we are reflections
Of our best men

Our women of honor
A story still unfolding
Wonderful chapter after chapter
Of a boy and a girl
And the vow of a lifetime

3.

A celebration of sorts
On this day, way back then
It was the eve of my wedding day
I wrote her proposal poems
Drank Talisker and smoked cigars
And now on this day, the annual eve
Before our anniversary
It's Gatorade and a Cuban
A fist full of poems sent away
So not much has changed
Save for the depth of my love
There's that I'm celebrating
On this day
& on the morrow

4.

Down the end
Of the long way
Water and sky
Something shimmers

From memory mixed with desire
And I stop to rest in the quiet
Saying, yes my brother
She's beautiful and bright
Today your daughter takes the walk
Down the marriage mile still
With you in her smile
Oh how the quiet reminds
Me my brother
Of your pride
And of your joy

5.
These two
Us
Three sometimes four
Immigrants and first gens
In a station wagon seeing
Sea to shining sea
What there was to see
Of our new homeland
As I shuttle my family
Of immigrants and dogs
On summer vacation
Exhausted finally arriving
Safe sound happy
I think of these two

What they did
For
Us

How It Goes

Here's the thing
    Teacup tendrils
    Kitchen window light
I'm not a story
Teller of ancient family secrets
Unearthed by me
    Dog slumbering by the fireplace
Not going to tell you
How to live
Your days in bliss
Rather simply point
This out
Or that and leave
It at that
You know
How it goes
    The house as quiet
    As church balconies
    Saturday nights
So, it goes
As the river flows
As they say
Me: oh look

There's a stone
To cross

Farewell to Kings

Walking home in the winter dark. A *Rush* album tucked under arm. Lemon-gin drunk at fifteen. Counting sluicing stars. The smell of sex on my hands, mystery on my tongue. A timber wolf there, a watcher on the tree-line. Those obsidian eyes. Making a choice not to defeat yet what haunted me, but shouting out my one true love's name before fleeing for my life. This is where I have felt most at peace -- alone at night in the winter, me & the cold, cold constellations dumb to the threat of violence and the cantus in my heart. Through the shining snow, dizzy and scared and piecemeal forgiven for thinking kings last. For forgetting is always forgiven

Observations During My Time as Christ of the Pots

Never place yourself anywhere near a cute child
When you are before an audience
Contrast is important.

Acting is reacting
Where sometimes audience is the play
Projection is required.

Post mortems are for patting actors
On the spine, only
The hottest place imaginable is not hell
It's the light booth.

Directors can read palms, scripts, but not minds
Funny one night is not the next
& don't fuck with props.

Actors are the center of attention
And they know it.
Good actors know who controls the center
Of attention.
Gifts are good.

Never wear flip-flops to an audition
For the stage is for performing
Murphy's Law -- the truth on stage is not
Necessarily the truth out there.

It's just more fun and well, dramatic.
Noises are difficult to time
Allowing one to understand
The unappreciated and the

Overly-indulged.
Best actors are nothing like their characters
Worst actors are.

Pee before the house opens
Remember something on stage
Looks stupid from off-stage looks
Entirely important and dramatic on stage.

There is no improvising lights and sound
If you are under qualified to run any technical part
Of a play, but highly qualified in another area of life.

The status from the former elevates slightly the latter
When someone on the crew discovers this status
Juxtaposes with poses.

Plays must have beds
Someone must have cancer.
Hint a lot about sex.

Mention Hitler
Mention Freud
Mention sex thrice.

Look into the audience, but don't look at them
Try not to show them your booty
Don't eat garlic
Before a performance kiss.

Smoke if you want
For flubbed lines is an opportunity to react
Second hand smoke is reacting in acting.

The run of any production:
Seemingly increases or decreases
Depending on your part
And wear underwear under your underwear because

Timing is everything.
Timing is everything.
Timing is everything.

Say everything three times.

Panes

Three panes: Father, Son, and The Holy Ghost; a past, a present, a future. Trinity wedged between outside and inside. A priest once told me a window doesn't concern itself with the past nor does a window concern itself with the future. It just fogs up when in the chill of morning a scream reaches towards it, the effect of trinity is an obscured view. For a moment, blissful blindness, then clarity. But always a barrier, a pane, between now and the next now. Always a son, one day a father, at least a ghost of empty sockets and forgotten facial gestures. There is no behind for a window, just ahead, a see-through. This is now, God's Occam's Razor, a present to edge through.

My voice bleeds on the pane.

Runs; Come back. Don't go. Come back. Into the present, a future leaves the past behind.

Breaks

Every day is a break, an examination of the break
between or from the previous and the to be.
From whom you might have been to who you are. It is a
break from the past.
It is breakers on a beach, constant, breathing and
crashing. A bonfire on the beach.
A remembrance of what has transpired and what we can
hope to achieve, should we allow the now to unfold as it
should, as it wants.
Walking, thinking and drinking in the air. The smells of
fresh dirt, oil and orange. Cleaners and containments.
The sound of birdsong, incessant and beautiful, the din of
people and cars and lives and wonders.
The black seam and the bright orders. The light filled
with the visible and invisible. The dance between these.
And those. There can be no words, but only the
mechanics of a body moving through space and time
toward what cannot be fully known or understood from
position of distance.
Inside and outside. The realm of the liminal. It is a daily
battle, and if not battle, then struggle and if not struggle,
then ascent, and if not that, a movement with the
shoulders.
I have no idea but this: I am here and it is now.

Nubivagant: a memoir (excerpt)

1.
Over the rim
      ceramic coffee mug
         those waves
      these clouds
         the shoreline
where my ruins ebb
   flow
      alight.

2.
To verb a noun
      we summer
         here.

3.
The anniversary porch
   perched near the sea
   water our sign
   of bondage.

Years ago on a cliff
overlooking the home of a lake monster
    We wed.

4.
Close your eyes.
    Faith.
Hold hands.

5.
It's very difficult to
label my feelings.
        A professor misses his students.
        For a concentrated period so close. So
important. Then it's over.
        And this happens
        every nine months. Year in
year out.

6.
Make it yours
        worry not theirs.

7.
Hold her hand.
        Hold it right now.

8.
Even the unfamiliar can
come to feel familiar. Like a
home.

9.
Let time go.

10.
Ships on the horizon
        move unseen across at night
        in the wavering shimmer by day
        both illusions of our stability.

11.
Some things are too complex
to label
        or to guide for being
too quick.
One minute all there,
            then not.

12.
This is not our home
        neither is where we call
        home. Instead

we carry it with us.

13.
No matter the dog gate
        the dog goes through
            the one
            security loop.

14.
Cicadas susurrant
        symphonic thrill
over-meshes the constant
        din of island traffic.

15.
Lines in a pocket journal
        riven by low tide wind,
        high tide current.

16.
The realist painter
Coville
wasn't after a direct
reflection of reality but
one shot
        through his luminist
            lens.

17.
So much depends
        on your parents
        what they set out
            to do.
Mine
immigrants to a new country
            already in motion
                    as it were, and simply
                        kept
                                moving
because what's familiar to them is not
a home
            for this is what they left
                but heart
which they carried
            when they left.

18.
Pelicans are passage
            land in the sea
                    a paragraph.

19.
Sea foam

spun sugar
water fluffy.

20.
Tattoos on the tanned.

21.
Parasurfer slices the waves
making a tiny wake.

22.
Eight-months pregnant
a halcyon around her
belly button.

23.
Very windy Pazuzu
from Savannah's midnight
garden.

24.
Overcast comes quickly
on little cat paws.

25.
Here take this
she said

Placing a wooden
        crucifix
around my neck.
For when you're in
        the water, the sea,
                it will float all
                        around you.

26.
The metal detectors
        all look
                the same.

27.
Varicose-veins
        make the old
                woman's legs look mightily
bruised.

28.
Nothing stops her from the ocean
edge. Not her wheelchair. Not the lack
                of a second leg.

29.
The singular self is the world
suffused with billions of

possibilities.

30.
Or
infinite sources of energy
        and sea.

IV.

1.
That's what I used
        to think
                then   I died
And rose from the dead.

2.
Three red-headed girls in a
        row
A covenant?

3.
Things are doable
        Martin and Dale say
                If you do them.
4.
Sometimes I speak

Polish

And she hears Spanglish.

5.

My shrugging

shoulders

are in almost constant

pain.

6.

Memory

folly of the mind

comes in waves.

7.

Striking

falling

away.

8.

Tomorrow –

Yoga, some work

the art museum we write

on the shoreline.

9.

Begin with happiness...

10.
Betwixt and besides
        Just those words. Not much
Else.
        All awkward.
        But all we've got.
        Betwixt.
        Besides.
        Being.
        Belonging.
        Be.

V.

1.
This is a sincere and serious
        question. How did you make
        peace
                with the quiet life?

2.
Suicide ideation
        enact in the mind
burns exhalation to the blackest
        sadness soot.

Inhaling rekindles life
    a flame
        of remembrance.

3.
It takes one to know
    one
    just ask
    me.

4.
You're home free
    as soon as no one
knows where to find
      you.

5.
If I could live my life over I
    wouldn't be
      in such a hurry.

6.
Not smelling roses. I
    mean getting
    to know myself.

7.

Something might have stuck.

Beautiful Disorder

This is how it goes
Up downs a chaos grows
Like madness, voices heard
Inside my head a caged bird

Oh, wonderful escapes
A fumbling staggering traipse
Undetected for so long
Hidden in me all along

The fantastic feats
Days of nothing but downbeats
Of two minds miasmic milky essence
An unknown known mere presence

Losing jobs losing friends
Not aware how of starts and ends
Years under doctor's tender care
Medications, sleep, incessant prayer

Finally coming to some terms
Twists, uncertainty and turns
Beauty in the disquiet borne
Of self forever twice torn

This is how I am naked
A being fettered and invaded
Nothing to plead and apologize for
There are windows and there are doors

This is the beautiful disorder
Poetry, ubiquity and complex order
Gazing out windows hopeful still for
Sometimes I walk through open doors

Emily Sings One

Emily sings the one
Without words lifting my hope
Of flight over fear
In the fugitive year

Every afternoon we convene
Birds of that plumage of feathers
In the swelter of summer
Magi, mystics and mummers

Prayer at the invisible altar
Deliverance for all lost or found
No sparrow without another
One and all sister and brother

This too shall pass we nod
Over our coffee and cigars
On the other side of the war
The end of tumult seemingly too far

We listen to Emily warbling
The one without words
Feathers to give us majestic flight
Over and through the enduring fight

Hope is indeed a thing
Within the breastbone of the mask wearers
Doing it for the years to come
When the we see where hope arrives from

Awake

Awoke to find all the windows open wide
Knowing this the day you're long gone
No easy thing seeing the mourning star
Starting to move into light and absence
Saying one day we'll see each other again
Maybe so, maybe so, the song goes
There's no mystery being born people do it
All the time, but this closing, all the windows
Might be the greatest puzzle of all
Our passion for having, finds peace
In our ache, for giving it all away

Broken

We fit each others pieces
The way dovetails require no steel
Together better loneliness ceases
Saying not what we ought, but how we feel

The way dovetails have no need of steel
For every jigsaw there are fit pieces
No matter how spent & vulnerable we feel
Together the mysterious puzzle ceases

For every jigsaw there are sound pieces
Gestures of trial, error and joy
Together the puzzle as problem ceases
To rob us of our beautiful envoy

Gestures tried error fading into joy
We cannot continue to live in a severed state
Which robs from our friendships, its envoy
Not pieced together spaces breed hate

Continuing to suffer separately
Folding into another humbly
To continue living severed, agitated state
Not a puzzle that which grows is hate

For broken, each of us, fit each others pieces

39

Curious Dogs

(after Sarton)

Because I want mostly permanence
I wander these hills at night
Drop my hands in the silver river
Sing to dawn's marching trees.

Because I want mostly happiness
I never open envelopes with a knife
Carry stones in my pockets
Fear running into you out on errands.

Because I want mostly contentment
Reading between the lines has dimmed
All the old newspapers scattered overboard
New shoes tied with old knots.

Because I want mostly emptiness
I never heard from you again
Feel my legs grow thick with thrumming worry
Whisper to myself the words can't have it all.

Because I want mostly not to want
Bury my recalcitrant bones

Some fissure on an ancient map
Unmarked and unremarkable left to be.

Found only much later by curious dogs
Their dumbfounded owners marveling
Over my bleached cleanliness.

Daphne

If I should wistfully stare
Wander loose in wild wood
It's first love
—Daphne
Pulling me again there.

Running ahead of me heavy still
Even though we lost her long ago
Hair tattered ribbons of gold
My voice after her thin, shrill.

Of course she is nowhere and everywhere
All at once the first and lasting
Impression upon a new heart
Sinking anew with each new stare.

Calling out to her fleeing
Wanting to keep Daphne mine
She slips the bonds
Of this earth titling, reeling.

That day in the forest cathedral
Ahead of me, and disappearing
Into what? A beautiful apparition of leaves

Seed borne magical wherewithal.

Even now, as when echoes my name
—Apollo
I wander through dark woods wondering
Did you find me?
Or did I find you all the same.

Ahead of me lost
Forever first love Daphne
Leaving me to stare and wander
Woods wild host

Among those ruinous trees
Numerous beauties
I still feel you near
In all that a man sees.

Mnemosyne Drinks to Korsakoff

You witness again with unction and bleary pleasure
Supreme achievements of distant sexual congress
Using inebriated harmonies, fumblingly gathered
Folds, family comes but not the one you remember
Raising another round to oh what is it?

For Cal drinks absinthe sucking a silver spoon of its
sugar
Droning dirges caffeine Clio scratches blood from her
flimsy skin
Accompanied by staggering Euterpe's ill-woozy flute
From the window, Meth Mel yawps but no one
Bothers your thoughts of whatsitsname?

Erato's stoned gaze considers the hocked lyre, consoled
By a green-gilled Poly, surging, heaving bones
Under adjudicating glow-in-the-dark stars U coughs and
spews
Goo into a stained snot rag, me gasping, grabbing
Aching swollen ribs, not disturbing some drowning
whatchamacallit?

Bottle after sweaty tumbler lugged by hags dressed like

mealy magpies
Slurring dumb Karaoke lyrics falling from your numb
Lips. You slowly, then – suddenly – well...
Too drunk to go on, Mummy
To tell me where you stashed car keys or how to holler
up Dad.

The Line

In the juggle of twist and salvation
We know hate, we know death
Always air thick with fear, the arid smell
Pain rising a fist with every sun.
Scrolls and tracts are fingered, messiahs
Messages presaged, foretold, forewarned.
What is written in hefty stone—
This is my house, get out; try and move it.
This is my land, step off; try to move me.
Stasis umbilicus paper and fire. Blood.
What is rare, is lightness when all is
Grievous and inconsolable—
Levity in a ferocious line
 Of sand and people in a Middle Eastern dust
 Storm. Of Jews on one side
 Palestinians bluster on the other.
 Each erasing with stubborn boots
 The line. Crossing each other on the
 Way seldom meeting. Never seeing each other
 Eye to eye.
 Each speaking their Deity's tongue
 Language of loss buried deep belief—
 This is the land of a thousand generations
 Suns rising over fields of blood feud. And yet—

Visited by three supermodels, on a photo
Shoot, near a newly erected barrier more
Than 450 miles long. Centuries sunk.
Leaning haughtily neutral in couture glad
Rags beneath a flourish of Arabic graffiti.
Nearby Allah schoolboys snicker, point all knowingly—
Not at exposed cleavage as one would expect, but at
The script coming as plainly as Quranic verse:
I am a Big Donkey.
Mute models sashshay while a photographer continues
The shooting.

Ovid Bonfire

Into the beach pit fire went
Ovid
His *Ode to Love* curling
Smoldering in the glowing pyre
We sat in our low back chairs
Wet glasses of whiskey
Tinny Edith Piaf — *Hymne A l'amour*
Watching embers lift
Disappear in tepid sea
Air burnished along with
Our lifting laughter
A poetry transformed
Though the conflagration
Wasn't entirely
Necessary the burning
In our chest testament
Enough —
Love & whiskey burns